ELECTRICITY AND MAGNETISM

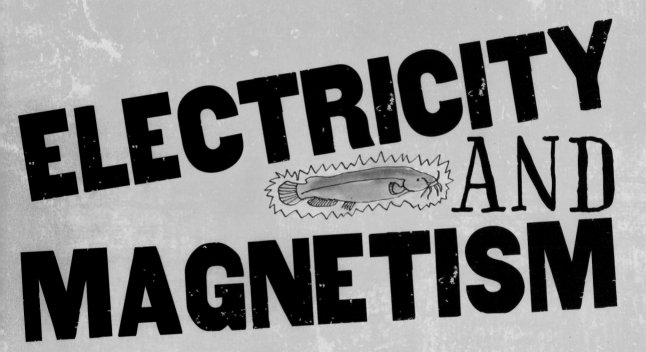

Anna Claybourne

Illustrated by Chrissy Barnard

First published in paperback in 2016 by Wayland

Text copyright © Wayland 2016
Illustrations © Wayland 2016

Dewey number: 537–dc23
ISBN: 978 0 7502 8971 9
Library ebook ISBN: 978 0 7502 8831 6
10 9 8 7 6 5 4 3 2 1

The rights of Anna Claybourne to be identified as the Author and Chrissy Barnard
to be identified as the Illustrator of this Work have been asserted by them
in accordance with the Copyright, Designs and Patents Act, 1988.

Series editor: Victoria Brooker
Series design: Lisa Peacock

A CIP catalogue record for this book is available
from the British Library.

Wayland is an imprint of Hachette Children's Group
Part of Hodder & Stoughton
Carmelite House
50 Victoria Embankment
London EC4Y 0DZ

Printed in China

An Hachette UK Company
www.hachette.co.uk
www.hachettechildrens.co.uk

Contents

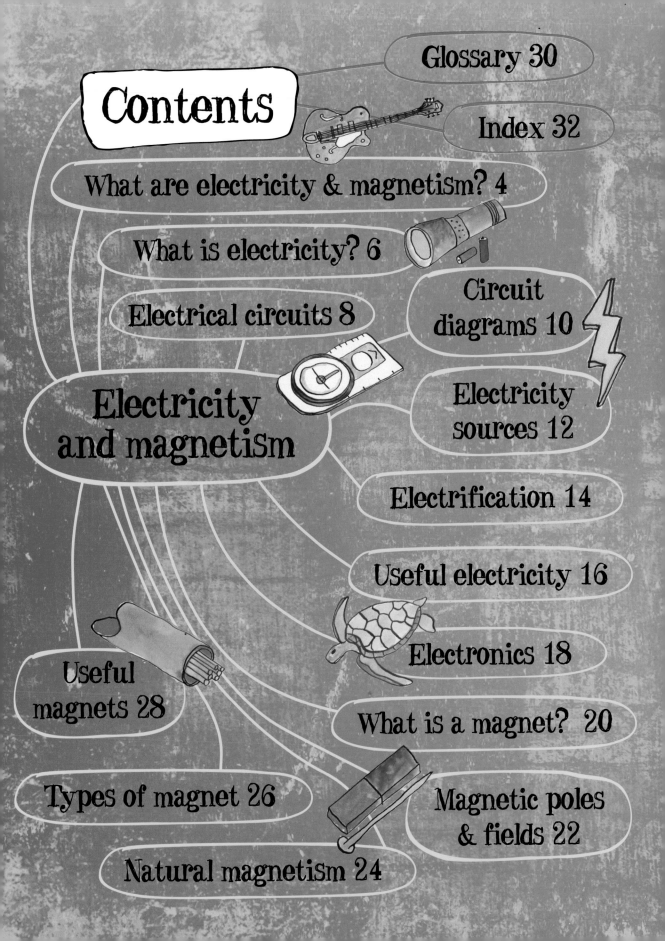

What are electricity and magnetism?

Electricity and magnetism are both important areas of science. They are central to many of the machines, inventions and gadgets that have been invented, and which we now rely on – from the light bulb and the compass to modern music systems, phones and computers.

Electricity

Electricity is a form of energy. Energy means the power to do work or make things happen. Electrical appliances, such as fridges, laptops and dishwashers, work when electricity flows through them, making them move, heat up or glow with light. Lightning is a huge spark of electrical energy that occurs naturally.

Magnetism

Magnetism is a type of force. You can feel this force as a pull when you hold a magnet close to a metal object that the magnet is attracted to. Magnets can also have a pushing force. When you hold two magnets close to each other, they sometimes push each other apart.

Electricity and magnetism

Although electricity is a form of energy and magnetism is a force, they are related. A flow of electricity creates a magnetic force, and a moving magnet can create a flow of electricity. Electromagnetic waves, such as light and x-rays, are a combination of both.

What is a mind web?

A mind web is a useful way of laying out the basic facts about a topic.
You put the topic title in the middle, and arrange words and ideas
to do with that topic around it. You can then draw lines linking
each of these to more words and facts that relate to them, along
with little pictures. Mind webs can also be called mind maps,
spidergrams or spider graphs.

A mind web shows you all the parts of a topic and how they link
together at a glance. It's a great way to sort out ideas and remind
yourself of everything you need to remember about a subject.

This mini mind web shows you the main topics to do with electricity.
You will find bigger, more detailed mind webs about each of them
in the rest of this book.

Sources

Uses

Electronics

Circuits

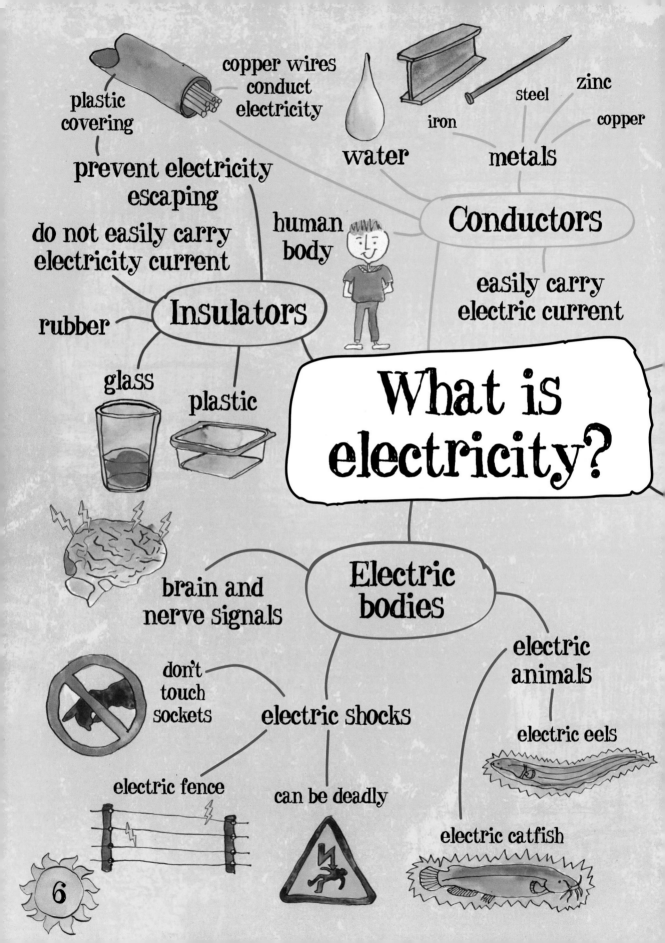

copper wires conduct electricity

plastic covering

water

iron steel zinc copper

metals

prevent electricity escaping

human body

Conductors

do not easily carry electricity current

easily carry electric current

Insulators

rubber

glass

plastic

What is electricity?

brain and nerve signals

Electric bodies

don't touch sockets

electric shocks

electric animals

electric eels

electric fence

can be deadly

electric catfish

6

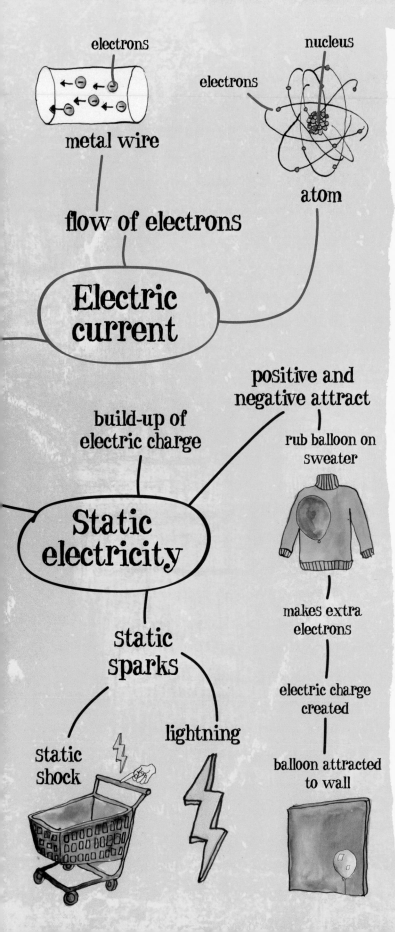

electrons

metal wire

flow of electrons

nucleus

electrons

atom

Electric current

Static electricity

build-up of electric charge

positive and negative attract

rub balloon on sweater

makes extra electrons

electric charge created

balloon attracted to wall

static sparks

static shock

lightning

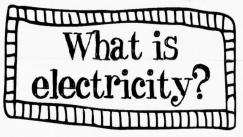
To understand electricity, you need to know about atoms — the microscopic building blocks that everything is made of. Atoms contain tiny parts called electrons. Each type of atom has a number of electrons whirling around it.

Electrons can separate from atoms and move around inside materials. This flow of electrons through a material is called an electric current. Only some materials, mainly metals, carry or conduct electricity easily. They are called electrical conductors. Materials that don't conduct electricity easily are called insulators.

Static (or 'still') electricity happens when a material collects or loses some electrons. This gives it an electric charge that makes it attracted to other materials. If a conductor touches it, electrons will flow between them until they are balanced out again. This is what creates static electric sparks.

Electric circuits

Current electricity can only keep flowing if it is in a loop, or circuit, connected to a battery or other power source. The power source provides energy in the form of electric charge. This makes electrons flow around the circuit. The parts of an electrical circuit, such as wires, batteries and bulbs, are called components.

Real-life circuits

All electrical appliances and gadgets, like TVs, torches, laptops and hi-fi speakers, can only work when they are part of an electrical circuit. As electricity flows around the circuit and through the device, it is converted into another form of useful energy, such as light, heat or movement. For example, as electricity flows through a light bulb, it makes it glow with light.

Off and on

As long as the circuit forms a continuous loop, electricity can flow around it. But if there is a break in the circuit, the current stops. A switch is a component that can break and reconnect the circuit to turn a device off and on.

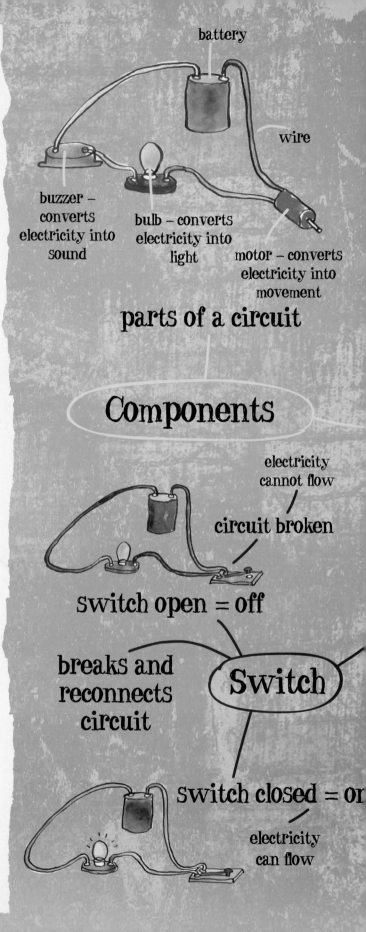

battery

wire

buzzer – converts electricity into sound

bulb – converts electricity into light

motor – converts electricity into movement

parts of a circuit

Components

electricity cannot flow

circuit broken

switch open = off

breaks and reconnects circuit

Switch

switch closed = on

electricity can flow

electricity flows
around

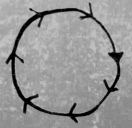

flow of electrons

flow of electricity
makes bulb work

wire

circuit

battery

Loop

Electrical Circuits

cylinder
battery

coin or
button
battery

batteries

car
battery

terminals

Power source

wind
turbine

other power
sources

mains socket

solar
panels

linked to
power
station

postive
charge

negative
charge

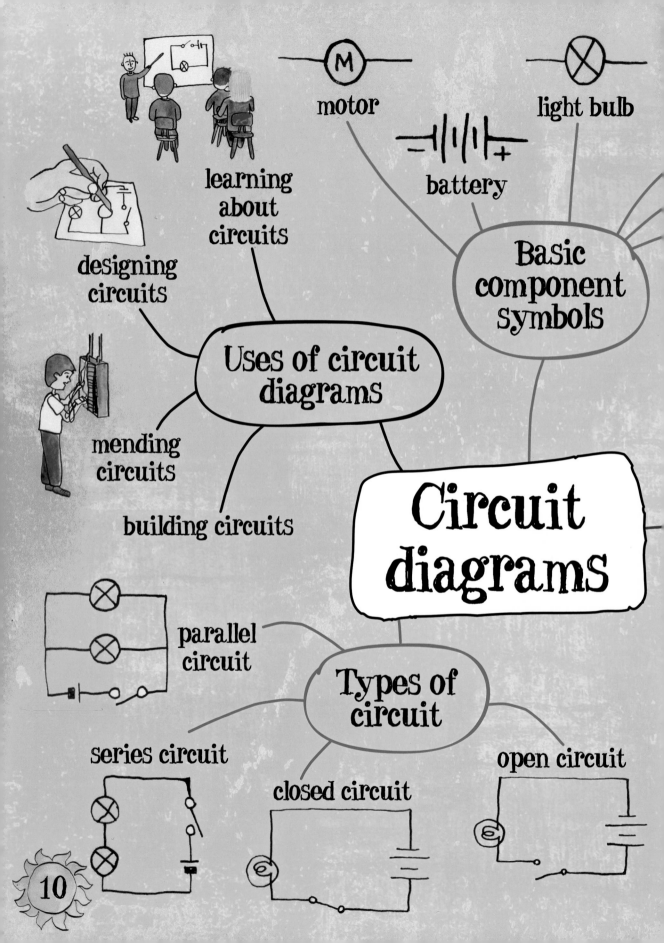

motor

light bulb

battery

learning about circuits

designing circuits

Basic component symbols

mending circuits

Uses of circuit diagrams

building circuits

Circuit diagrams

parallel circuit

Types of circuit

series circuit

closed circuit

open circuit

10

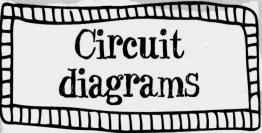

Circuit diagrams

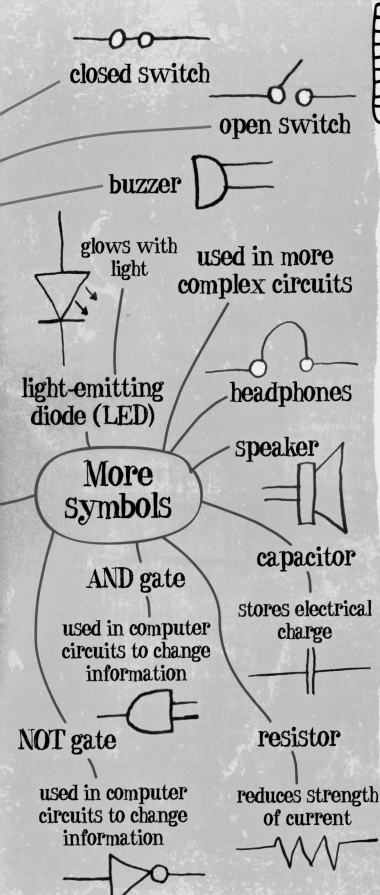

closed switch

open switch

buzzer

glows with light

used in more complex circuits

light-emitting diode (LED)

headphones

speaker

More symbols

capacitor

AND gate

stores electrical charge

used in computer circuits to change information

NOT gate

resistor

used in computer circuits to change information

reduces strength of current

Circuit diagrams are used to show an electrical circuit and all its parts clearly. Instead of simply drawing a picture of the circuit, the diagram uses a clear symbol for each type of component, such as batteries, bulbs and motors. Most of the symbols are recognised around the world, meaning that everyone can share and understand the same diagrams. Circuit diagrams can be simple, like the ones shown here, but some – such as those showing the workings of a computer – can be very large and complicated.

What are they for?

Circuit diagrams are useful in lots of ways. They are used in schools to teach students about different types of circuits and components and what they do. They are also used to teach trainee electricians about circuits. In the world of work, they help electrical engineers to design circuits for electrical appliances. People who build or fix the appliances can also follow the diagrams to help them find the right parts.

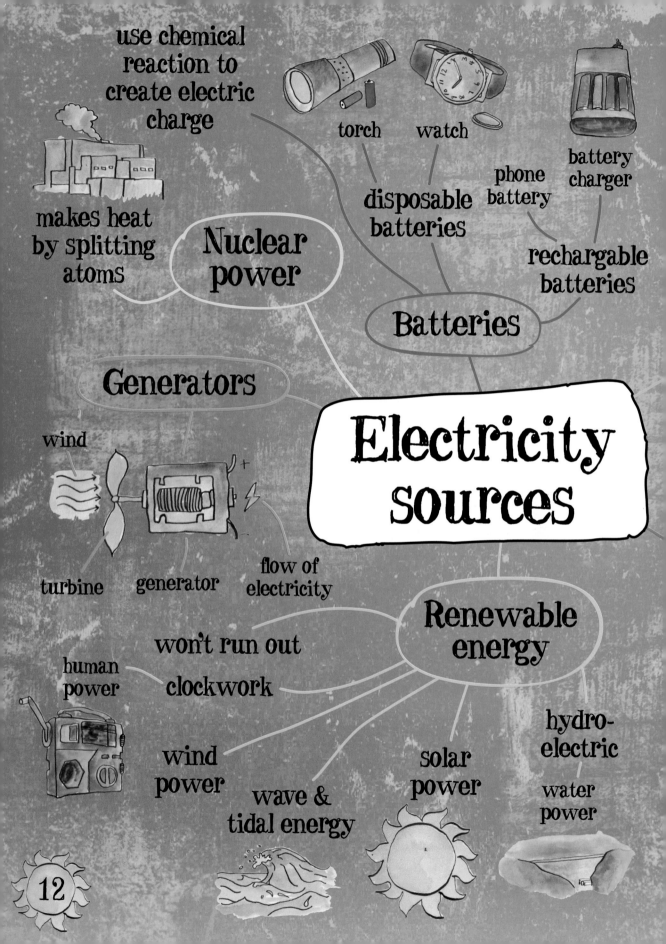

use chemical reaction to create electric charge

torch   watch

disposable batteries

phone battery   battery charger

rechargable batteries

makes heat by splitting atoms

Nuclear power

Batteries

Generators

Electricity sources

wind

turbine   generator   flow of electricity

Renewable energy

won't run out

clockwork

human power

wind power

wave & tidal energy

solar power

hydro-electric

water power

12

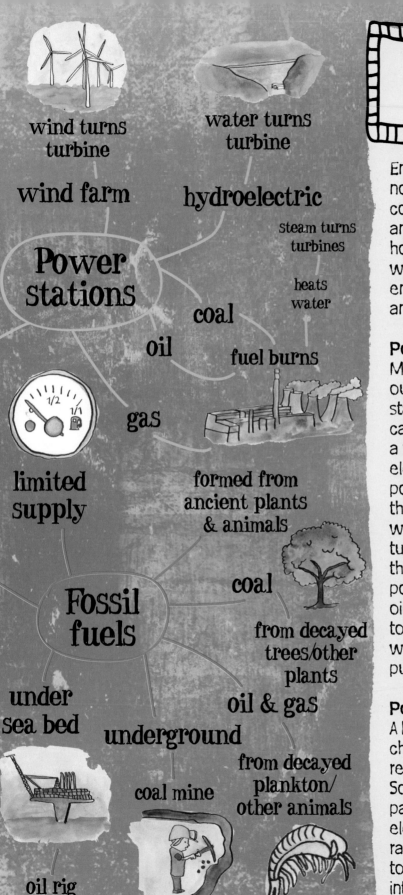

wind turns turbine

wind farm

water turns turbine

hydroelectric

Power stations

steam turns turbines

heats water

coal

oil

fuel burns

gas

limited supply

formed from ancient plants & animals

Fossil fuels

coal

from decayed trees/other plants

oil & gas

under sea bed

underground

coal mine

from decayed plankton/ other animals

oil rig

Energy cannot come from nowhere – it can only be converted from one form into another. To get electricity for our homes, factories and gadgets, we convert other forms of energy, such as movement, heat and light, into electrical energy.

Power stations

Most of the electricity we use in our homes comes from power stations. They use machines called generators, which convert a rotating movement into an electric current. At hydroelectric power stations and wind farms, the power of flowing water or wind makes a wheel called a turbine rotate, and this makes the generator work. Other power stations burn fuel such as oil, coal or gas, or gather sunlight, to make heat. The heat boils water and makes steam, which pushes the turbines around.

Portable supplies

A battery holds a store of chemical energy that can be released as electrical charge. Some calculators have a solar panel that turns sunlight into electricity, while clockwork radios and wind-up torches turn movement into electricity.

13

Electrification

Electrification means bringing an electricity supply to streets and buildings. The electricity travels from the power station along networks of cables and wires. These have to be kept safe so that they can't give people electric shocks.

Cable network

The biggest cables carry electricity at a very high voltage and are very dangerous. They can be buried underground, or held up out of reach on high towers, called pylons. The electricity in these cables is too powerful to use at home. So the cables lead to electricity substations where the voltage is reduced. You can probably spot a substation somewhere near your home. They are usually small buildings or enclosed areas marked with danger signs.

In your house

From the substation, smaller underground mains cables lead along streets and into houses. In each building, the cables lead to a central fuse box. Here they split into circuits that carry electricity into different rooms.

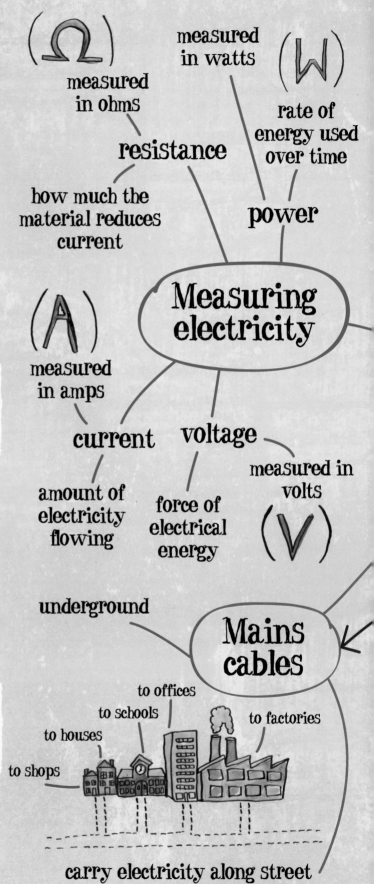

(Ω)

measured in ohms

measured in watts

(W)

rate of energy used over time

resistance

how much the material reduces current

power

Measuring electricity

(A)

measured in amps

current

amount of electricity flowing

voltage

force of electrical energy

measured in volts

(V)

underground

Mains cables

to offices

to schools

to factories

to houses

to shops

carry electricity along street

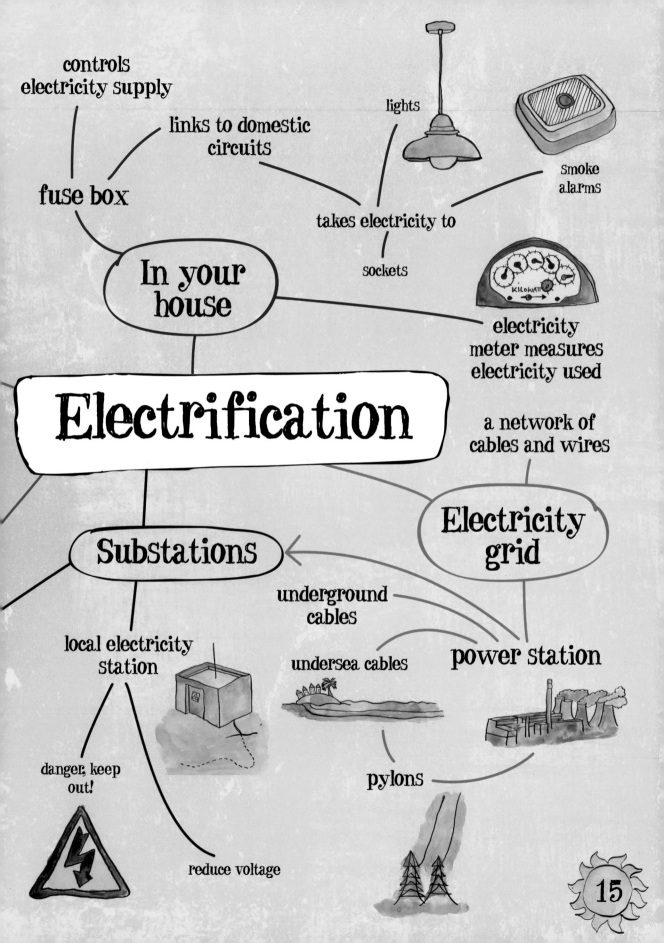

controls
electricity supply

links to domestic
circuits

lights

smoke
alarms

fuse box

takes electricity to

In your house

sockets

KILOWATT

electricity
meter measures
electricity used

Electrification

a network of
cables and wires

Electricity grid

Substations

underground
cables

local electricity
station

undersea cables

power station

danger, keep
out!

pylons

reduce voltage

15

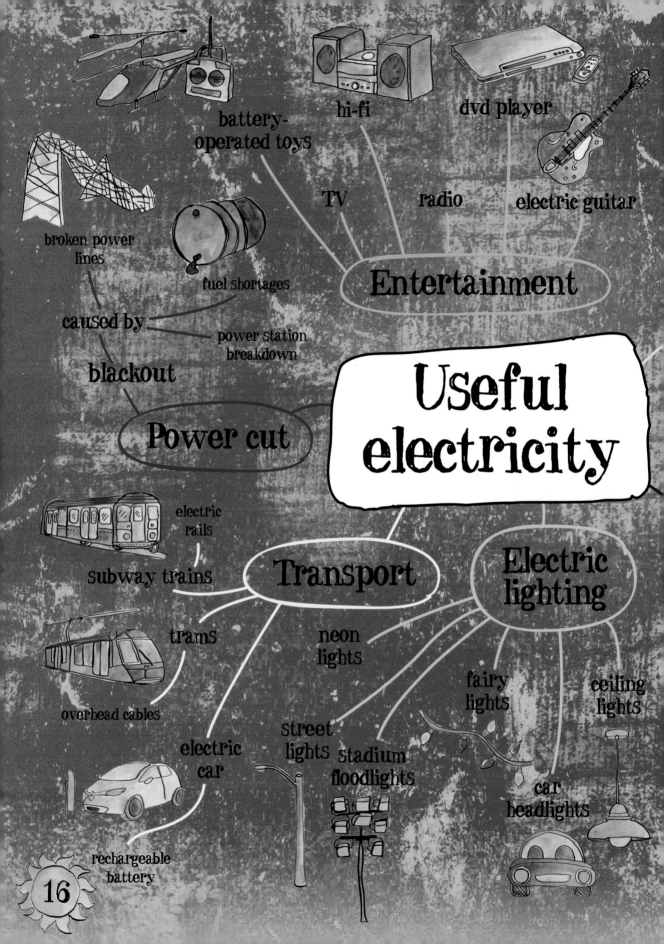

battery-operated toys

hi-fi

dvd player

TV

radio

electric guitar

broken power lines

fuel shortages

caused by

power station breakdown

blackout

Entertainment

Useful electricity

Power cut

electric rails

subway trains

Transport

Electric lighting

trams

neon lights

fairy lights

ceiling lights

overhead cables

electric car

street lights

stadium floodlights

car headlights

rechargeable battery

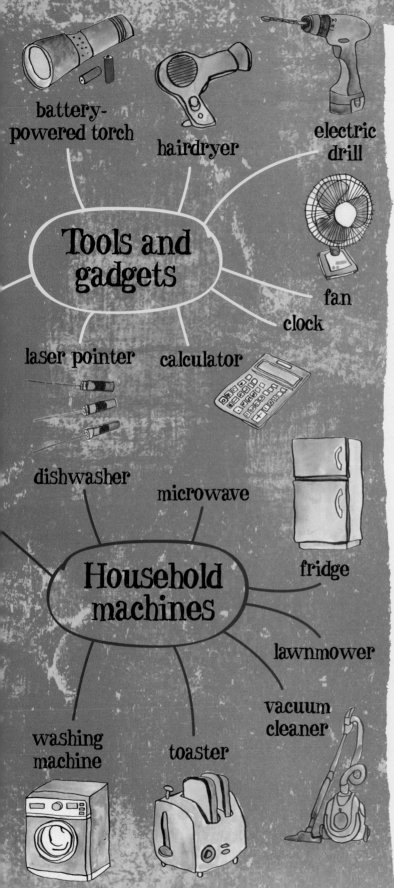

battery-powered torch

hairdryer

electric drill

Tools and gadgets

fan

clock

laser pointer

calculator

dishwasher

microwave

fridge

Household machines

lawnmower

vacuum cleaner

washing machine

toaster

The modern world depends on a steady supply of electricity. We have thousands of electrical gadgets, tools, and machines for doing housework and having fun. Most buildings, roads and vehicles have electric lighting. Many trains, buses and cars run on electricity. Workplaces and banks need electricity to power their machines. Our systems for moving money around, sending messages and making phone calls are all electrified too.

Blackout!
If the electricity was suddenly switched off, there would be chaos. This does sometimes happen, when power stations go wrong, or bad weather cuts off supply cables. It's called a power cut or blackout.

Energy shortage!
Luckily, most blackouts only last an hour or two. However, the fossil fuels used to make electricity are starting to run out, so power cuts could become more common.

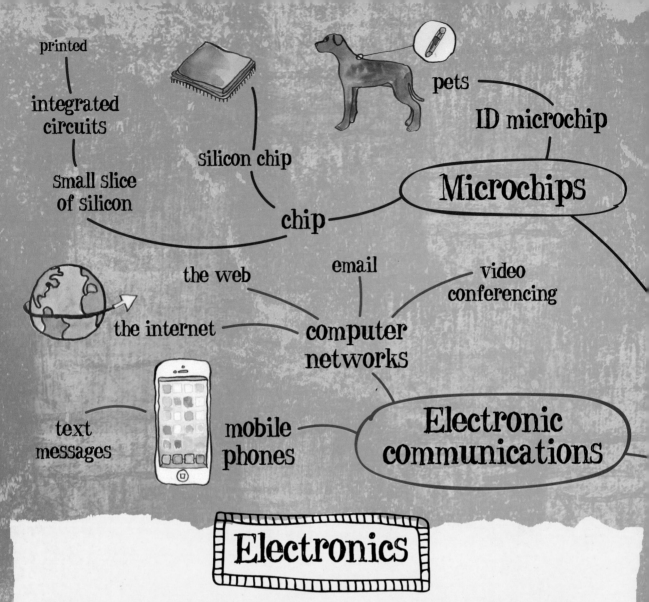

printed

integrated
circuits

small slice
of silicon

silicon chip

chip

pets

ID microchip

Microchips

the web

email

video
conferencing

the internet

computer
networks

text
messages

mobile
phones

Electronic
communications

Electronics

Electrical machines and appliances use electricity to power them – but there's another, extremely important way we use electricity, called electronics. Instead of just using electricity as power, electronic devices use the flow of electricity around a circuit, or the changing strength of an electric current, to store information, send signals and do calculations. Electronic devices have very complex circuits that make electricity flow along many different pathways and switch tiny components on and off. This process is what makes computers work, along with many other electronic devices. They are often called digital devices because they work using digits, or numbers, stored inside the circuits.

Over time, we have found ways to make electronic circuits smaller and smaller. Modern digital devices contain tiny flat microchips, usually made of a material called silicon, with microscopic circuits printed onto them. The first computers were big enough to fill a room, but there are computers small enough to fit in your pocket.

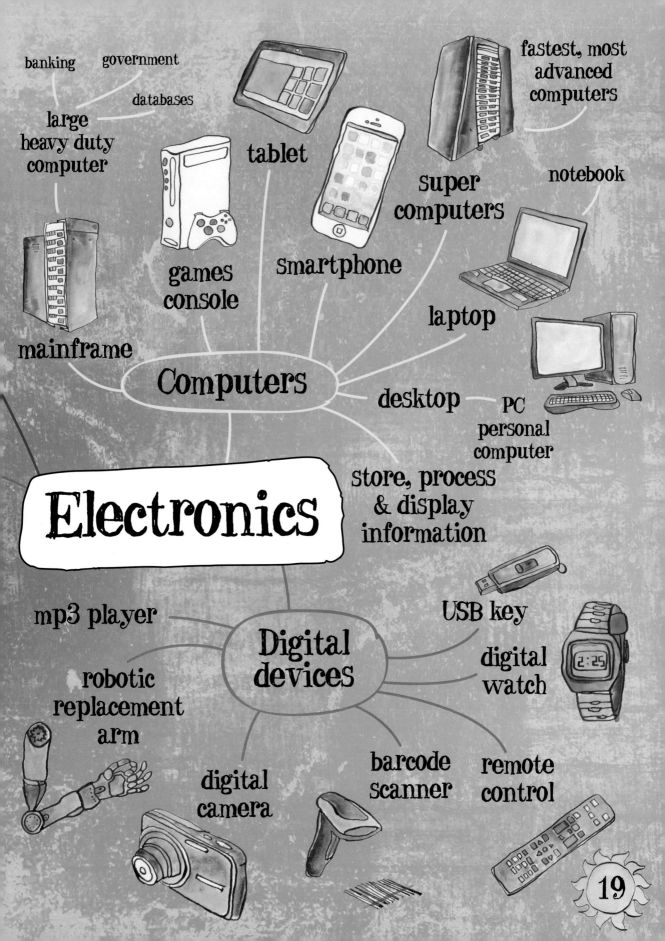

banking   government

databases

large
heavy duty
computer

tablet

fastest, most
advanced
computers

super
computers

notebook

games
console

smartphone

laptop

mainframe

Computers

desktop

PC
personal
computer

store, process
& display
information

Electronics

USB key

mp3 player

Digital
devices

digital
watch

robotic
replacement
arm

digital
camera

barcode
scanner

remote
control

19

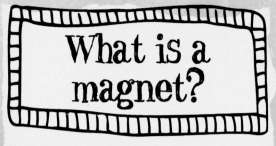

What is a magnet?

Magnetism is a type of force. You can feel this force if you hold a magnet near an iron or steel object, such as a paperclip. The magnet attracts the paperclip and pulls on it. Only a few materials can be attracted by magnets, or made into magnets. They are called ferromagnetic materials, and are mostly metals. They include iron, steel, cobalt, nickel and the mineral magnetite. The atoms (tiny building blocks) in these materials contain loose electrons that create a pulling force. They create tiny magnetic areas inside the metal, called magnetic domains. In a magnet, the domains are all lined up in the same direction, giving the whole piece of metal a pulling force.

Electricity and magnetism
Electricity and magnetism are closely related. They both work because of the way electrons in metals behave. It's possible to make a magnet using an electric current, and vice versa. Magnets are a vital part of generators, which turn movement into electricity, and motors, which turn electricity into movement.

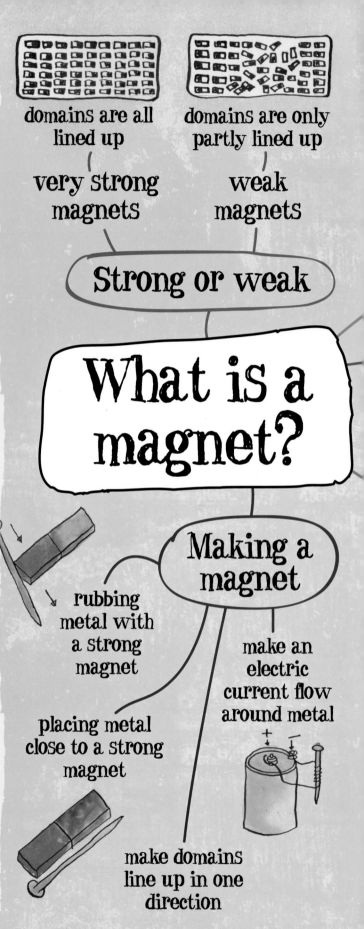

domains are all lined up

domains are only partly lined up

very strong magnets

weak magnets

Strong or weak

What is a magnet?

Making a magnet

rubbing metal with a strong magnet

placing metal close to a strong magnet

make an electric current flow around metal

make domains line up in one direction

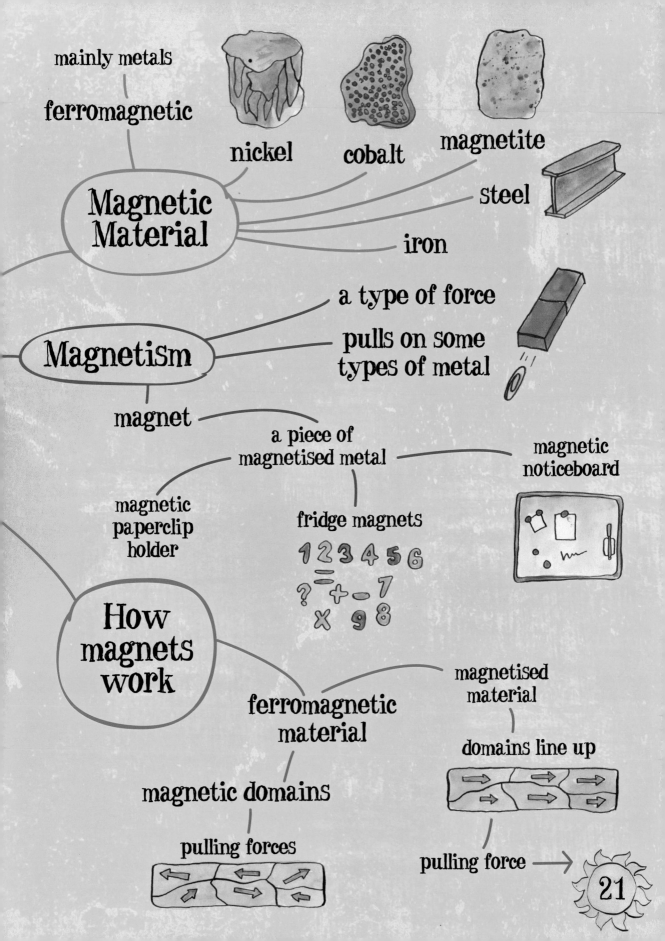

mainly metals

ferromagnetic

nickel   cobalt   magnetite

Magnetic Material

steel

iron

a type of force

Magnetism

pulls on some types of metal

magnet

a piece of magnetised metal

magnetic noticeboard

magnetic paperclip holder

fridge magnets

1 2 3 4 5 6
? = + - 7
× 9 8

How magnets work

ferromagnetic material

magnetised material

domains line up

magnetic domains

pulling force

pulling forces

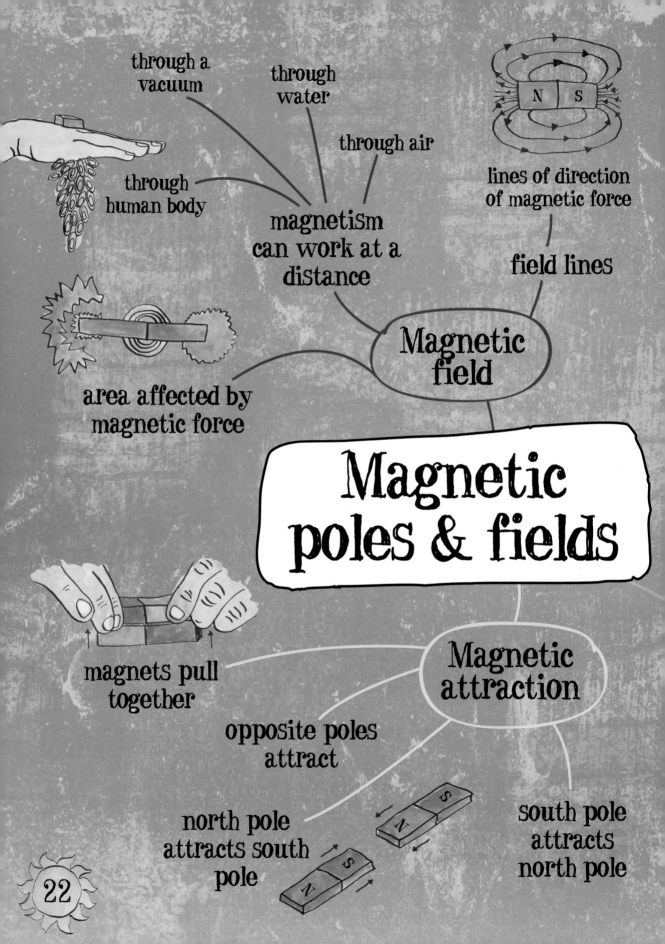

through a vacuum

through water

through air

through human body

magnetism can work at a distance

lines of direction of magnetic force

field lines

Magnetic field

area affected by magnetic force

Magnetic poles & fields

magnets pull together

Magnetic attraction

opposite poles attract

north pole attracts south pole

south pole attracts north pole

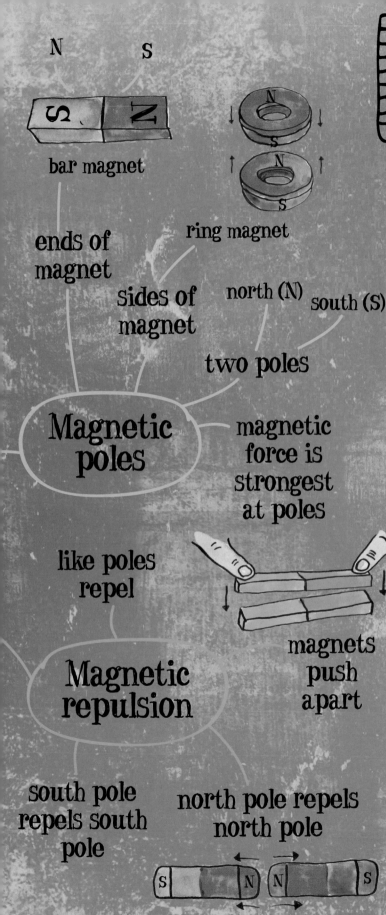

N   S

bar magnet

ring magnet

ends of magnet

sides of magnet

north (N)   south (S)

two poles

Magnetic poles

magnetic force is strongest at poles

like poles repel

Magnetic repulsion

magnets push apart

south pole repels south pole

north pole repels north pole

Magnetic poles & fields

A magnet has two opposite ends or sides (depending on the shape of the magnet), called magnetic poles. They are named the north pole and the south pole.

Attracting and repelling

Both a magnet's poles will pull a ferromagnetic material towards them. But if you put two magnets together, they will behave differently. A magnet's north pole and another magnet's south pole will be pulled together by the force of magnetic attraction. But if you put two north poles or two south poles together, they will repel each other, or push each other away, instead. This force is called magnetic repulsion.

Magnetic fields

A magnetic field is the area around a magnet that is affected by its magnetic force. The direction of the force changes as you move the magnet around. This can be shown as a pattern of lines, called magnetic field lines.

Natural magnetism

We can make magnets, but they can also occur naturally. This was how people first discovered magnetism. Natural magnets, known as lodestones, are magnetised pieces of the mineral magnetite. There is also another, much rarer, magnetic mineral, called pyrrhotite.

Magnetic Earth

Our planet, the Earth itself, is also a huge magnet, and has its own magnetic field and magnetic poles. Scientists think the Earth's magnetism is caused by the way molten metal swirls around inside the Earth's core. The North Magnetic Pole and South Magnetic Pole are quite near the geographic North and South Poles, but are not in exactly the same place. They gradually move around as the swirling metal inside the Earth changes position.

A compass works because its needle is a magnet. It will always line up with the Earth's magnetic poles and point north. Some animals also have a magnetic sense that tells them which way is north.

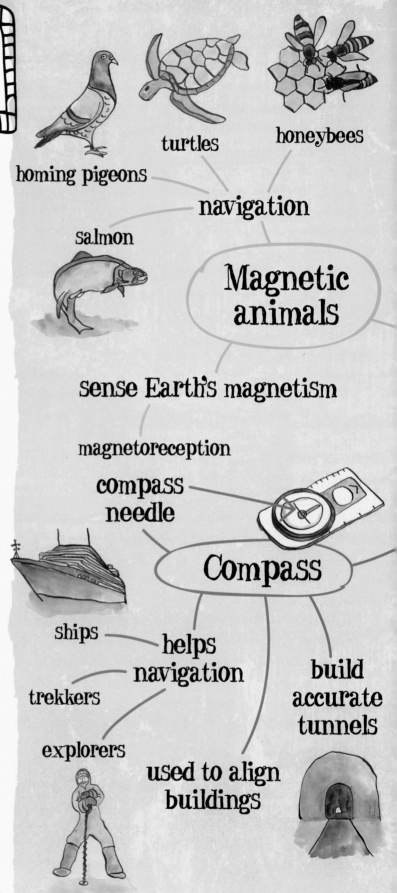

homing pigeons

turtles

honeybees

navigation

salmon

Magnetic animals

sense Earth's magnetism

magnetoreception

compass needle

Compass

ships

helps navigation

trekkers

explorers

build accurate tunnels

used to align buildings

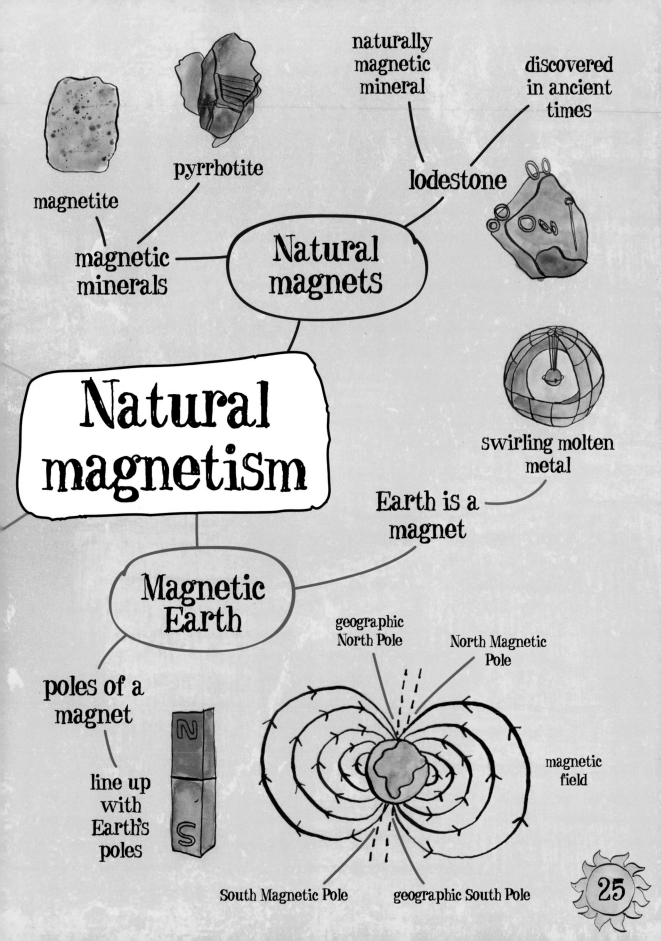

magnetite

pyrrhotite

naturally magnetic mineral

discovered in ancient times

lodestone

magnetic minerals

Natural magnets

Natural magnetism

swirling molten metal

Earth is a magnet

Magnetic Earth

poles of a magnet

line up with Earth's poles

geographic North Pole

North Magnetic Pole

magnetic field

South Magnetic Pole

geographic South Pole

Types of magnet

There are three main types of magnet. Permanent magnets are the normal, everyday magnets you might find in your home, for example in a toy or a fridge magnet. They keep their magnetism over time, and can be made in a variety of different shapes.

A temporary magnet is an object that becomes a magnet while it is touching a magnet or is in a magnetic field. For example, if a steel paperclip is touching a magnet, it will become magnetic itself and will be able to attract another paperclip. Once it is removed from the magnet, it loses its magnetism.

Electromagnets

An electromagnet is a spiral-shaped coil of wire with a metal core in the middle. It becomes a magnet when an electric current flows through the wire. This type of magnet can be switched on and off as part of an electrical circuit.

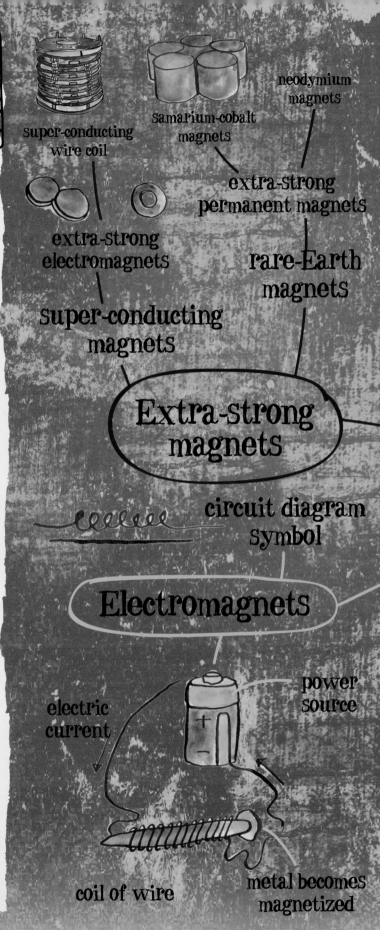

super-conducting wire coil

samarium-cobalt magnets

neodymium magnets

extra-strong permanent magnets

extra-strong electromagnets

rare-Earth magnets

super-conducting magnets

Extra-strong magnets

circuit diagram symbol

Electromagnets

electric current

power source

coil of wire

metal becomes magnetized

steel nail

needle

ball bearings

paperclip

ferromagnetic objects

iron filings

Temporary magnets

become magnetised when close to a magnet

Types of magnet

spherical

Permanent magnets

bar

rod

flexible tape

magnet shapes

ring or doughnut

horseshoe

disk

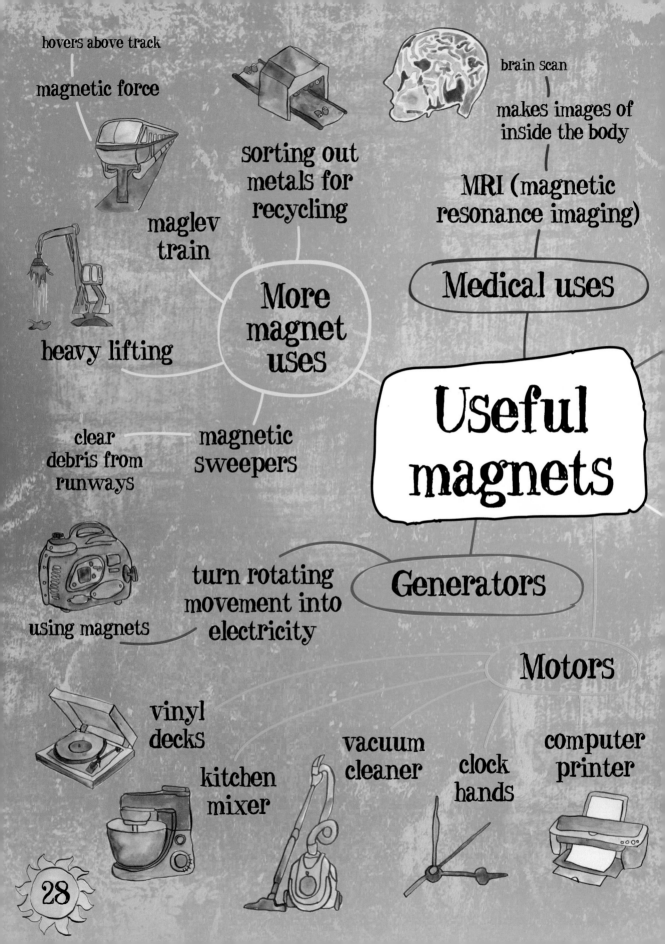

hovers above track

magnetic force

maglev train

sorting out metals for recycling

brain scan

makes images of inside the body

MRI (magnetic resonance imaging)

Medical uses

heavy lifting

More magnet uses

Useful magnets

clear debris from runways

magnetic sweepers

turn rotating movement into electricity

Generators

using magnets

Motors

vinyl decks

kitchen mixer

vacuum cleaner

clock hands

computer printer

28

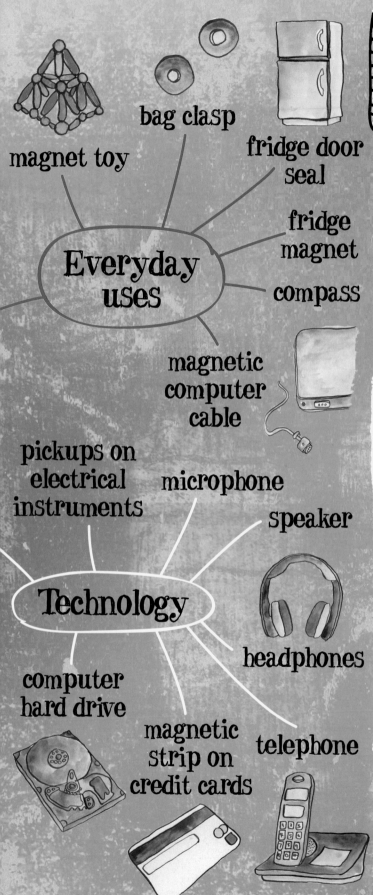

magnet toy

bag clasp

fridge door seal

Everyday uses

fridge magnet

compass

magnetic computer cable

pickups on electrical instruments

microphone

speaker

Technology

headphones

computer hard drive

magnetic strip on credit cards

telephone

We use magnets for hundreds of things. You'll find them in bag fastenings, key holders and around a fridge door to keep the fridge tightly closed. Computer power cords often have magnets to hold them in place.

Hidden magnets

Motors need magnets to make them work, so there are magnets in any gadget with rotating parts, like fans, food mixers and drills. They are also an important part of telephones, microphones, speakers and the pickups on electric guitars. In sound and video recording and computer hard drives, information is stored by making patterns of magnetic particles. Credit and debit cards also store data in their magnetic strip.

Mighty magnets

More powerful magnets are used to lift heavy metal objects or sort out different types of metals. Even the Large Hadron Collider, which makes particles zoom around in a circle to carry out experiments, depends on magnets to make it work.

Glossary

atoms Tiny units that materials are made of.

attract To pull towards.

blackout Darkness caused by loss of electricity supply.

circuit Loop of wire or other conductor that electricity can flow around.

components Parts of an electric circuit.

conduct To carry a flow of electricity.

conductor Material that can conduct electricity well.

core Innermost part of the Earth.

digital To do with information held in the form of numbers.

domain Tiny magnetized area within a magnetic material.

electrical engineer Someone who designs electric circuits and devices.

electric charge Build-up of electrical energy.

electric current Flow of electricity.

electrician Someone who builds, mends or maintains electric circuits or devices.

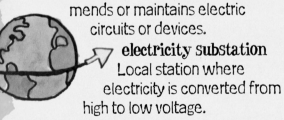

electricity substation Local station where electricity is converted from high to low voltage.

electrification Installing an electricity supply in streets and buildings.

electromagnet Magnet that is switched off and on using an electric current.

electrons Tiny particles that are found in atoms but can also move separately.

electronic Using electric circuits to store, process and control information.

energy The power to do work or make things happen.

ferromagnetic material Material that can be attracted by a magnet or become a magnet.

force A push, pull or influence on an object.

fuse box Control panel linking mains supply to the circuits inside a building.

generator Device that turns a rotating movement into a flow of electricity.

insulator Material that is poor at conducting electricity.

lodestone Naturally occurring magnet, usually made of magnetite.

magnetic attraction Pulling force of a magnet on a metal or another magnet.

magnetic field Area of magnetic force extending around a magnet.

magnetic field lines Lines showing direction of magnetic force in a magnetic field.

magnetic poles Ends or sides of a magnet where the magnetic force is strongest.

magnetic pyrite Another name for pyrrhotite.

magnetic repulsion Pushing force between the matching poles of two magnets.

magnetite A naturally occurring ferromagnetic mineral.

mains The electricity supply delivered to houses and other buildings.

microchip A slice of silicon with with tiny electric circuits printed onto it.

motor Device that turns a flow of electricity into a rotating movement.

North Magnetic Pole The Earth's natural magnetic pole that is nearest to the North Pole.

ore Naturally occurring rock or mineral that contains a metal or other useful substance.

permanent magnet A magnet that does not lose its magnetism.

power cut A loss of electricity supply.

pylon Another name for a transmission tower.

pyrrhotite A naturally occurring ferromagnetic mineral.

repel To push away from.

solar panel Device that converts light into a flow of electricity.

South Magnetic Pole The Earth's natural magnetic pole that is nearest to the South Pole.

static electricity Build-up of electric charge in a substance.

switch Electric component that can break or reconnect a circuit.

technology Inventions, tools and machines designed to solve problems and do tasks.

temporary magnet Object that only becomes magnetic when it is in a magnetic field.

terminal a device at the end of a wire or cable that allows a connection to be made to an electrical circuit.

transmission tower High tower supporting live electricity cables.

turbine Wheel used to turn a flow of wind, water or steam into a rotating movement..

voltage Measurement of electrical energy.

Index